W9-ADJ-782

LEAD [SIMPLY] Copyright © 2012 by Give More Media Inc.

All rights reserved. No part of this book may be reproduced or presented in any form or by any means without advanced written permission from the publisher. Duplication of any part of this book by any form or means is a violation of copyright law.

Lead [simply]™ is a trademark of Give More Media Inc. It also should not be reproduced in any way.

Published with love in Richmond, Virginia by Give More Media Inc. This is the 5th printing.

ISBN: 978-0-615-63699-3

804-762-4500
GiveMore.com/Lead

by Sam Parker

CONTENTS

EL.

NECT. N°2

LVE. N°3

THAT'S IT. Ridiculously simple.

THE FRAMEWORK

N°1 MODEL.

N°2 CONNECT.

N°3 INVOLVE.

That's your framework for leadership – your simple, day-to-day, in-the-trenches formula for creating that special team of people that does important and meaningful work … that cares to make things better … continually … every day.

Model the behavior you want to see.
Connect with the people you lead.
Involve them as much as possible.

That's it. Ridiculously simple.

THE FOUNDATION

For many years, The Gallup Organization has conducted surveys and polls to help us understand how into our work we are. The fancy term for this in the study of organizational behavior is **employee engagement**.

They've determined the following (give or take a percentage point one way or the other depending on the year)…

$\frac{29}{100}$ - - - - - ● **of us are engaged with our work (we care)**

$\frac{54}{100}$ - - - - - ● **are not engaged with our work (we don't really care)**

$\frac{17}{100}$ - - - - - ● **are actively disengaged with our work (we really don't care … and we spread it … we thrive on getting in the way of making good things happen)**

Call the first group what you like (start with wonderful but then realize that being engaged in our work is really just our obligation to each other). The last two groups are Gomos and D-grunts. Gomos are the people who go through the motions. D-grunts are the disgruntled among us.

Add the two groups together and we have 71 out of every 100 people going through the motions each day… or worse.

FRIGHTENING, ISN'T IT?

Think about that lost potential (unrealized potential).

(Do the math. What's your experience?)

Why would more than half the people who go to work every day leave their hearts and minds at home? Why would so many people be so apathetic about their work? Hundreds of variables that could come into play here, right? Many of them are far beyond our control as leaders.

Perhaps, though, one of the most basic points behind all of it is that too many of us have forgotten that we're ultimately doing what it is we do so that we can make good things happen for other people.

Walk that **basic mission statement** through every single role, every single profession, and every single industry and you'll see that it fits.

→ WE'RE HERE TO MAKE GOOD THINGS HAPPEN FOR SOMEONE ELSE. WE DO THAT ... **AND IT ALL WORKS.**

So as leaders (with a title or not), how can we help the people around us (and ourselves) remember that and be more likely to stay engaged (wonderful)? How can we be sure we don't lose all that valuable time and energy and the fulfilling enjoyment of service (contribution, care) and the great results all of it can bring (organizationally and personally)?

First, we need to accept the fact, as challenging and frustrating as it might be, that the need for solid and ongoing reinforcement never (ever, ever, ever, ever) ends.

Think about that. To become stronger or more skillful in anything, we have to **commit to continual training and practice.**

I LEARNED VERY VERY EARLY ON THAT YOU CAN BE VERY VERY TALENTED **BUT IF YOU DON'T TAKE CARE OF YOUR TALENT, IT CAN GO AWAY.** IT'S LIKE A BIG BABY. IT NEEDS TO BE FED.

ANNIE LEIBOVITZ
American photographer

How comfortable would you be with your surgeon if she only practiced medicine at an annual weekend retreat?

Think about working out. What positive results can we expect by visiting the gym just twice a month?
(Of course, some of us continue to try.)

Learning a musical instrument or better golf game – everything we want to get better at and everything we want to be sure doesn't atrophy, erode, or degrade requires ongoing attention, effort, and practice.

Why do we forget this? It should be the reverse. As we get more and more experience, we should get wiser and remember it more often as we face our challenges in leading other people (and ourselves). We need to (and please hear this)…

BE AS **COMMITTED AND CONSISTENT** IN OUR COACHING AND DEVELOPMENT EFFORTS AS WE ASK **OUR PEOPLE TO BE** IN THEIR ROLES AND WITH THE PEOPLE THEY SERVE.

(Did you hear that?)

Leadership is **a joint effort.**

We need to support each other more often and remember our interdependence and our obligation to the big picture…

We're here to make good things happen for other people.

This is what will help us grow that engaged minority (that 29% of people who care) into the engaged majority. This is what will help us create incredibly productive teams and relationships of high-trust and truth (much more enjoyable) instead of being content with something less because it's uncomfortable and difficult to push ourselves.

(uncomfortable = growth)

THERE ARE RISKS AND COSTS TO A PROGRAM OF ACTION. **BUT THEY ARE FAR LESS** THAN THE LONG-RANGE RISKS AND COSTS OF COMFORTABLE INACTION.

JOHN F. KENNEDY
35th U.S. president

You see, if we consider ourselves to be in that engaged minority, we have an obligation to help bring other people over to the bright side of things – to bring the Gomos over. (What about the D-grunts? See the More Thoughts, Sources, and Resources section in the back of this book.) And then the ultimate goal is to have those people start caring enough to encourage the people around them to be more engaged through **their actions** and through **their words**.

And there's your holy grail of leadership…

PEER-TO-PEER
ACCOUNTABILITY.

I once had the opportunity to talk with a Top Gun instructor (the U.S. Navy's training program for exceptional pilots). He shared with me that the goal of the program isn't just to create an elite group of pilots that stands separated from everyone else, but rather it's to **send out teachers** – teachers who go back to their units and help others improve as well.

That's the joint effort and deeper commitment to the big picture we need – surrounding ourselves with more and more engaged people and people who care about making good things happen – cultivating an environment that makes this possible.

CULTIVATE: (VERB)
TO NURTURE THE GROWTH OF

(what a wonderful word)

That's the opportunity we have with the people we lead. And here's the twist…

If we don't try to create a high-trust, highly accountable environment as leaders – if we give up going for the creation of a special team of people who do "amazing amounts of important work" and try to be "stunning colleagues"* – **then we, as leaders, are the Gomos**.

(This would be a good time to pause and reflect. Is it possible this is our big picture problem with everything? Could it be what stands in the way of more customers, revenue, profit, contribution, and enjoyment?)

So, what can/should we do … today … **right now?**

MODEL. CONNECT. INVOLVE.

* These phrases are from the Netflix organization. See the More Thoughts, Sources, and Resources section for more on their inspiring culture.

TO HELP A YOUNG SOUL, ADD ENERGY, INSPIRE HOPE AND BLOW THE COALS INTO A USEFUL FLAME ... THAT IS THE WORK OF DIVINE MEN [AND WOMEN].

RALPH WALDO EMERSON
American writer and activist

MODEL

Commit to being engaged yourself, regardless of circumstances.

Be what it is you want to see more of.

Think about what it is you'd like to see from your team and model it.

More enthusiasm. Less cynicism.

More results. Less busyness.

More objectivity. Less wishing and guessing.

More focus. Less distraction.

More approachable. Less eggshells.

More patience and kindness. Less grumpiness.* (next page)

More encouragement. Less withholding of encouragement.

More appreciation. Less entitlement and neglect.

More listening. Less telling.

More truth. Less half-truths, omissions, and exaggerations.

More creativity. Less mediocrity.

More pursuit. Less passivity.

More humility. Less ego and politics.

More time, effort, and care.

Whatever you feel is most important to making a better experience for everyone (and achieving great results), model it. No exceptions. Fall off the horse? The moment you realize it, apologize (to others and yourself) and get back on it.

Not comfortable acknowledging your mistakes and apologizing? You've got company. But doing so (authentically) makes you more human (and that's what you are, right?) and can help you create that higher level of internal trust you're hoping for (which leads to those better relationships and better results you want).

Remember...

WE LEAD BY EXAMPLE –
ONE WAY OR THE OTHER.*

* See the Modeling Ideas section for some specifics.

Grumpy

Such a childish word, isn't it? Fitting given it's such a childish behavior. Be careful not to dismiss its impact because it can get in the way of everything and it can spread. And when it spreads, it impedes work. And when work is slowed or hobbled, everyone loses.

"TREAT YOUR PEOPLE AS YOU WOULD WANT YOUR CUSTOMERS TO BE TREATED."

LEE COCKERELL
former EVP of Operations,
Walt Disney World

CONNECT

Connect = Talk. Listen. Show. Share.

Have more frequent, intimate, and meaningful conversations about what it is you and your team do and the value you and your team bring to the world.

Show people the big picture more often. Share any external feedback you get from the people you serve (good and bad). Share it as much as possible in order to help people be more connected to that big picture (your purpose … your raison d'etre – that's French for your reason for being … sexy, huh?).

Let people know you have their back and appreciate them. Tell them. Show them. Encourage them. Thank them. Do it in person and do it in writing.*

Consider a quick daily team meeting (some organizations call it a daily huddle) that allows everyone to share what they're working on and any challenges they're facing. This will help people feel more connected to each other

---

* See the Modeling Ideas section for some specifics.

and each other's work. When we're more connected to each other (personally), we feel better about each other, more accountable to each other, and have an easier time supporting each other (you want people supporting each other … peer-to-peer accountability, right?). You want to be sure you're encouraging an open flow of information between colleagues at all levels. **Contact is where you hear things** (sooner rather than later … very important). And be sure to rotate leadership of those meetings to increase involvement, empathy, accountability, and to keep the tone fresh (new leadership = new tone). Add some regular team lunches or dinners to the mix to make even more personal connections.

Your relationship with your team (and their relationship with each other) is incredibly important to creating an engaged, accountable, and results-focused team of people (and an environment that people are drawn to and don't want to leave). Study after organizational behavior study shows that (do we really need another study to tell us relationships are important?*). Connecting with people is how you will learn more, inspire more, and encourage people to make more useful things happen.

IDEA

Periodically, remind people how many hours you and your team are putting out into the world each day (multiply the number of people on your team by 8) and what the possibilities are for that amount of time (e.g., the people you can help and what that means).

* See the Modeling Ideas section for some specifics.

IDEA

Remove or limit inter-office instant messaging and email communications. The viability of removing either will depend upon what kind of environment you have. The spirit here is to encourage real-world personal contact that leads to better relationships, more personal accountability (no hiding out), and faster action.

Email and instant messaging can be a distraction and create confusion (see the **MORE FOCUS** thoughts in the Modeling section in the back of this book). The written word without a face or body language can be misinterpreted very easily. And, because people recognize they can be misinterpreted in what they write, they may spend more time "crafting emails" than it might take to simply talk with someone.

IDEA

Make it a point to let people know you're interested in them (professionally and personally). Ask them how you can help them with the issue they're facing on that project or with that near-term objective. Allow them to share more about that personal thing they're interested in. Do it in person where possible but also by email and text (a little contradictory to the previous point but that idea is more about limiting our dependency on electronic communication that can separate people from each other).

" WHAT IT MEANS IS, IF I'M A MANAGER AND I WANT TO GET BETTER, AND I WANT MORE OUT OF MY PEOPLE AND I WANT THEM TO BE HAPPIER, TWO OF THE MOST IMPORTANT THINGS I CAN DO

IS JUST MAKE SURE I **HAVE SOME TIME FOR THEM** AND TO **BE CONSISTENT.** AND THAT'S MORE IMPORTANT THAN DOING THE REST OF THE STUFF. "

LASZLO BOCK
SVP of People Operations,
Google

INVOLVE

You want stronger people (future leaders)? You've got to involve them more in solving the challenges you face.

Wherever possible, let your people lead the effort to make that something special happen. Let them see things from your vantage point (a better view) so they're better informed and have a better chance at solving problems … with you (and eventually without you).

Ask people more frequently to give you their thoughts on things (good and bad). Ask them how they would change things if they were running the show. Then listen (really). When we're more involved in something and more accountable for something, generally speaking, we're more engaged. Do whatever you can to help make people feel **personally responsible for results** and serving the people you serve.

Let them know that you're involving them because you're interested in their development and in them becoming more valuable to the organization. If you've created that high-trust environment and those high-trust relationships, let them know you're helping them practice and perfect their abilities so they're valuable no matter where they are – not just with you (a good thing to remind them of when things get really challenging on a particular project or initiative). You want to develop people who shine when they go elsewhere (other departments, other companies, other industries).

IDEA

Sit down with your team and create a list of the things each of you would like to see more of at your organization (together). To get things started, you could use a couple of the points from the list in the Model section of this material. This will help people feel more involved and encourage more commitment to the effort.

The key to all of this really comes down to caring about the people we work with - involving them the way we'd like to be involved if we were in their shoes - treating them the way we'd like to be treated.

Not rocket science (like most things)…
just the golden rule.

Model the behavior you want to see.
Connect more with the people you lead.
Involve them.

That's it.

LET'S GO TO WORK >

How many 1-second opportunities do you have each day?

1-second opportunities to model the behaviors you want to see.
1-second opportunities where you choose to make a personal connection.
1-second opportunities where you help someone be more involved.
1-second opportunities where you send everything in the right direction.

MODELING IDEAS

These ideas might be valuable for everyone on your team. Share what you like. But the point of the list is to model the behaviors ourselves, as leaders.

MORE ENTHUSIASM...

A simple challenge where everyone wins (you and those around you). No risk. No additional time required.

Within the next 3 weeks (or maybe the next 3 minutes), set a 2-day period as your days (or your team's days) to inspire others. Two days where you'll put on blinders to anything negative and be the one in the office who everyone else can count on for words and actions that inspire and encourage. Two days where you're the light for other people – your colleagues, your customers, your patients, your students – no matter what.

Allow nothing negative and focus only on your service to others ... **only on your service to others** (worth repeating).

Once you set your 2 days, fully commit to the effort regardless of the inevitable challenges, regardless of the weather (please, never the weather). Fall off the inspirational horse at 2:11 on the first day? Get back on at 2:12 – no excuses.

Remember, you wake with an option for your daily attitude. Challenges will come up regardless.

Choose positive. Spread it for two days. Spark a habit.

MORE FOCUS...

What would it look like if you and your team really focused on a consistent basis?

You'd likely…

- » Contribute more
- » Waste less time ramping back up
- » Serve customers better (internally and externally)
- » Find more customers
- » Come up with more ideas
- » Plan better
- » Be less frustrated and stressed
- » Help others focus more (interrupting them less)
- » Make more money (for everyone … including you)

Nothing's guaranteed, of course. But it's a better bet. (And in the long run, you'll enjoy more.)

5 WAYS TO KNOCK OUT THE BULK OF DISTRACTIONS...

1. **Establish focus hours** with your team (or company-wide) – chunks of time each day where everyone will allow everyone else to focus (that includes you). No inter-office communications unless it truly can't wait. Ours at GiveMore.com are from 10 am – 12 pm and 2 pm – 4 pm (4 total hours a day). You'll make mistakes occasionally and break focus hours but with commitment and reinforcement, everyone will benefit. If you're really tough, in order to minimize outside distractions, let your family and friends know your focus hours (and turn off your cell). They'll love you for it – eventually.

2. **Turn off email alerts and commit to checking it at the most minimal level** you feel is possible for your particular world without having a negative impact on service. Most of your inbound emails are probably important but still don't need attention for at least an hour (if not longer). Be truthful with yourself and set your interval so everyone wins. If you can set only two or three specific times a day to respond to email, do it. Consider having an

auto-responder that lets people know when you address your email (e.g., "Thanks for your note. I usually check my email three times daily (8:30 am, 11:30 am, 4:30 pm). If you need me immediately, please call my cell / assistant / office line.").

(See the More Thoughts, Sources, and Resources section for what we learned at GiveMore.com by doing this - page 57.)

3. **Turn off instant messaging and chat services** unless your work absolutely requires it to get the job done (key word – absolutely). Having to phone someone or talk with them live (by visiting them) will make you more aware and respectful of someone else's time (and yours). And everyone's time is important. Be careful with it. Once it's gone, you can't get it back.

4. **Avoid the web during your money hours** (your most valuable time at the office) unless you absolutely need it for your work. The distractions are endlessly wonderful for those who'd prefer to avoid making good things

happen (which of course, isn't your goal). If you must open a browser during your money hours (or focus hours), make sure your home page is something that doesn't have the potential to encourage you down ~~destruction~~ distraction road (e.g., news or email sites, social networking sites, personal favorites). Search and discover outside your money hours or at lunch.

5. **Face away from distraction** (the door or other people – not customers, of course) if you're in an office setting that allows you to do so.

Depending on your team, some or all of these ideas might not go over well. Involving people in a discussion, asking them for ideas on how to improve internal focus and minimize distractions might be a good first step (**model, connect, involve**). Also, consistently helping people remember the purpose behind what it is you do for your customers (that big picture) can help you gain commitment to those reasons to focus.

MORE APPROACHABLE...

How much kinder would we be if we knew, at the end of the week, we'd be shown our 5 ugliest moments toward other people ... on film?

(This is my approachable look at the office.*)

What's so sad about not being approachable is that it can get in the way of everything. 1-second and we can change the mood completely ... shutting down ideas, feedback, information, and enthusiasm that can lead to the results, margins, profits, and progress we're all looking for.

To get where we want to be, to move forward is a joint effort between people. We need to get rid of the eggshells and be available to each other (happily). That's how work gets done.

---

* I'm kidding. I posed for the shot above to illustrate the point. Unfortunately, it wasn't hard to get in the moment though – too much bad practice. I'm working on it.

MORE PATIENCE...

Give people the time you'd like to be given.

(Simple, huh? See **MORE HUMILITY** on page 44.)

MORE APPRECIATION & ENCOURAGEMENT...

We all love encouragement and recognition (and most of us need it). But for some reason, we too often forget to give it.

3 ideas beyond the money (gift, medal, or trophy*)...

1. List the days of the week on a piece of paper (or on or in whatever gets your daily attention). During the day, be deliberate about encouraging one person and thanking one person (at least). Say it. Write it. Then write those names down next to the day (it could just be in your calendar of choice). If that gets to be too much, set a target of 3 or 4 names for each week. The point is to create a habit of gratitude and encouragement that feeds your relationships and makes things more pleasant for everyone. (You want that, don't you?)

---

* A medal or trophy? Please ... I'm kidding.

2. Use flip charts or whiteboards in hallways or entrances to publicly recognize people. Have fun with the language. Be real. Several (obvious and not so obvious) recognition opportunities…

Of course you'll want to use a different name if they're not Joe or Jennifer. (That's supposed to make you smile … as is the reference to the film "The Help" in the poster on the right.)

- » Welcoming (people coming back from a vacation or extended off-site meeting, new people on their first day)
- » Anniversaries (employment and personal)
- » Awards won (personal and professional)
- » Significant achievements (production goals, sales goals, quality goals, 1st speeches given, classes completed, 1st marathons run)

- » Meaningful risks taken
- » Significant displays of support for someone or some initiative (long hours, volunteering for something no one else wants to do, pushing something)
- » Birthdays
- » New children
- » Congratulations for children's accomplishments (graduation, college acceptances, awards)

A couple things to remember...

Missing someone for something you've recognized before with another person could create some bad feelings. That's where you get real and apologize (maybe even publicly).

Also, consider the personality of the person who's being publicly recognized and how they'll feel about it. If you predict a negative outcome, recognize them privately.

3. When you choose someone to take on a difficult project (or any project, really), be sure to let them know you've chosen them because you're confident they can make it happen (e.g., "I know you can do this. That's why I chose you. It'll be challenging but I've got your back.").

When someone's not hitting the mark or making something happen, confirm your expectations and commitment to them. Point out one or two very specific talents you know they have that can help them get there. If you can recall and share an example of where they were resourceful and resilient in the past (and it led to success), point it out. Ask them what they think. Give them the time and encouragement you'd like to be given.

MORE LISTENING...

Have you ever considered how ridiculous it is to talk over someone?

Why do we let it happen? Maybe it's the simple excitement over the discussion topic, poor listening training, ego ("Let me show you what I know instead of learning from what you know!"), or just plain rudeness.

Do you do it?

Ever cut someone off mid-sentence with...

"I don't mean to interrupt but..."
"Sorry to interrupt..."
"Oh, hey, real quick..."
"Wait..."

Here's one way to correct it…

Commit yourself to dropping a **small gap of silence** between what someone else says… and your response – just an extra beat or two. You'll be amazed at what else you learn and the better connections you'll make.

MORE TRUTH…

If you're not getting push back from time-to-time (or conversations aren't occasionally uncomfortable), you may not be getting the full truth. And without the full truth, your choices and actions might take you in the wrong direction.

Make sure you do your best to objectively dig for truth (rather than hope or wish something to be). **Ask that second and third question** that can open up new veins of information and deepen everyone's level of understanding (brutal truth).

Anything less and you're playing games.

(See the More Thoughts, Sources, and Resources section for one of my favorite stories on truth - page 58.)

MORE PURSUIT...

What if no one pursued improvement (personally, professionally, organizationally)? What if no one pushed it, risked it, and pushed it again (and again)?

Our world gets better because of those people who pursue that next step toward truth, development, and the way things could and should be.

What if more of us considered ourselves obligated to being a part of making a positive difference in the world? What if more of us stepped out of passivity (meeting expectations, apathy, indifference) and chose **the pursuit of better?**

Imagine how inspiring that would be to all of us.

(See the More Thoughts, Sources, and Resources section for more pursuit of pursuit - page 58.)

Questions that encourage pursuit...

Where do we want to be? Where should we be?
What do we want to do? What should we do?
What do we need to get there? Who do we need to get there?
How can we push it even further? What's next?

'YOU CAN'T START A FIRE WITHOUT A SPARK.**

BRUCE SPRINGSTEEN
American music artist

MORE HUMILITY...

We need to get out of the way of ourselves...
dumping that obtrusive ego ... remembering that
our job isn't to hold onto our position (double
meaning there). Our job is to improve things.

Imagine a world without ego (the bad ego ... the in-
flated sense of self-significance ego). There'd be no...

- » Toes to step on
- » Feelings to hurt
- » Fair shares to grab
- » Territory to defend
- » Fault to allocate
- » Back to watch
- » Last words to get
- » Ideas to hold back
- » Embarrassment to bear
- » Battles to win
- » Knowledge to prove
- » Entitlement to have
- » Encouragement to withhold
- » Credit to seek
- » Grudges to hold
- » Jealously to feel
- » Revenge to take
- » Hidden meanings to construe

Things would get done so much faster and so much more enjoyably.

Speak no ego. Be no ego…

1. **Be humble.** Understand you are a (small) part of the world. Service and patience should be your top priorities.

2. **Be teachable.** Focus on what you can learn, rather than showing what you know. Remember that almost everything you know began with the work of someone else.

3. **Listen more.** Make every effort to truly understand what others are saying (beyond just words). It makes for better connections. Remember that gap of silence (from the more listening idea). Ask questions (and listen, again).

4. **Appreciate people.** Enjoy others' contributions. Don't squelch ideas or defend territory. Encourage people more.

5. **Relax.** Let go of the need to be right or win every time.

MORE TIME & EFFORT...

Too many people lose productivity on a particular day of the week because of a Flintstone-like mentality* perpetuated by sitcoms and morning radio personalities. (For proof of some people's disdain for Mondays, search Twitter at 8am at the start of the week for the word "Mondays".)

In some places, Tuesdays are the new week. (Wednesday is hump day, Thursdays are almost Fridays, Fridays are practically the weekend and Mondays, they're for ramping up.)

It's time for a little luksa. (It's Polish for "let us kick some @$$." I'm joking again. It's an acronym I made up.)

Could you spark a little positive revolution and help someone break out of the TGIF mentality (or yourself if it applies)? How could you inspire a "let's kick some @$$" Monday morning start to the week?

Wouldn't both be more fun (and profitable)?

---

* What's a Flintstone? The Flintstones is an animated TV show that originally ran from 1960 to 1966. It's about the lives of "a modern stone-aged family." In the opening segment of each show, the main character excitedly stops and leaves work the moment the whistle blows.

Remember … Today is 20% of your workweek. To lose only two workdays a month to fatigue or a desire to wait for a better day to do something, would be to lose more than a full month of workdays each year (scary).

Imagine if your income or revenue reflected your slow days and know that in the long run, it probably does.

WHY LEAD [SIMPLY]?

When I think about most of the challenges we have in our workplaces, organizations, homes, and schools, I believe most of it's because we've forgotten to **give consistent day-to-day attention** to those simple things that have the biggest impact on making things better.

We've allowed ourselves to be distracted, chasing after complex solutions instead of embracing what's simple.

Why?

Maybe it's because we think the complex will be more interesting. Maybe it's that we think we want to be busy and we forget that what we really want is to be effective and contribute and make good things happen for other people (which leads to good things happening for ourselves).

I'm a big proponent of the "descending order of importance" approach to things. This means I believe that we should nail the most important things first and work our way down the list.

I don't live it like I'd like to, but I believe in it and that's my target.

Model. Connect. Involve.

3 little actions that can take care of everything else.

Not always easy … but definitely simple.

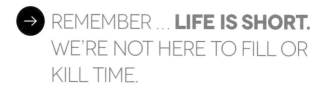 REMEMBER … **LIFE IS SHORT.** WE'RE NOT HERE TO FILL OR KILL TIME.

WE'RE HERE TO **MAKE GOOD THINGS HAPPEN FOR OTHER PEOPLE.**

MORE THOUGHTS, SOURCES, AND RESOURCES

Mission, vision, and values discussions are frequently mentioned in leadership material. Obviously important, but here I've chosen to focus on the leadership work that most managers and supervisors face every day (where the **real work gets done**). Creating, sharing, and living those missions, visions, and values comes from leading simply (modeling, connecting, involving).

Gallup's study I reference is called, "State of the American Workplace." It can be found at **GiveMore.com/Gallup**. I combined the results over the decade they reported on. Each year, the numbers move a few percentage points one way or the other but for the most part, they remain relatively the same (how sad). A little leading simply and maybe you can be a part of the small group of people who change all that (see the King quotation at the end).

If you need more studies or data to fully embrace the Model. Connect. Involve. framework, you can read the following (or you could invest that time right now in connecting with your people)…

» **Towers Watson Global Workforce Study.** Heavy, heavy for me … **GiveMore.com/TW**. They categorize people into 4 segments (rather than 3, like Gallup) – highly engaged, unsupported, detached, disengaged. Their results are equally scary.

» **Gallup's Q12 Meta-Analysis.** Another heavy read… **GiveMore.com/Q12**. For a more approachable (and enjoyable) presentation of similar material, read the book, "12: The Elements of Great Managing" by Rodd Wagner & James Harter (published by Gallup Press).

» **BlessingWhite's Global Employee Engagement Report.** They surveyed more than 7,000 people globally and have similar conclusions as the other studies. They put people into 5 groups – engaged, almost engaged, honeymooners & hamsters, crash & burners, disengaged … **GiveMore.com/BW**.

» **Psychometrics Engagement Study.** More interesting stats and thoughts based on a smaller survey of Canadian HR professionals… **GiveMore.com/PM**.

The "amazing amounts of important work" and "stunning colleagues" language is from Netflix (the organization … not a film). They put together a wonderful slideshow for potential employees called, "Netflix Culture: Freedom & Responsibility." It can be found at **GiveMore.com/Netflix**. It's a great read.

Leibovitz's quote is from the television series, "Visionaries: Inside the Creative Mind" produced by OWN (Oprah Winfrey Network). This 2011 episode profiled Leibovitz and her work. Inspiring. Oprah does some wonderful work. Yes … I'm a fan.

Kennedy's thought can be found in scores of books and periodicals.

D-grunts … If you have them (the actively disengaged) ask yourself why you're allowing them to be on your team and potentially getting in the way of your engaged people's work (and inhibiting the potential growth of any Gomos who are trying to get to the bright side). Out of patience and kindness, you might encourage a D-grunt to improve once (maybe twice) but then a change should be made. And it might be that change that helps them personally in the long run.

Emerson's statement is from his work "Society and Solitude" (chapter 11: Success). The words around the quote are also wonderful...

> Don't hang a dismal picture on the wall, and do not daub with sables and glooms in your conversation. Don't be a cynic and disconsolate preacher. Don't bewail and bemoan ... Nerve us with incessant affirmatives. Don't waste yourself in rejection, nor bark against the bad, but chant the beauty of the good.

> To awake in man and to raise the sense of worth, to educate his feeling and judgment so that he shall scorn himself for bad action, that is the only aim.

> 'Tis cheap and easy to destroy ... Yes, this is easy; but to help the young soul, add energy, inspire hope and blow the coals into a useful flame; to redeem defeat by new thought, by firm action, that is not easy, that is the work of divine men.

Cockerall's quote is from his book, "Creating Magic" published by Doubleday. Long for me but it's got wonderful leadership insights and reminders from how they lead at Disney.

Bock's thought is from the article, "Google's Quest to Build a Better Boss" published by The New York Times (March 12, 2011). Solid points backed up with Google data (and that's good data). It includes the 8 good leadership behaviors they identified and the 3 pitfalls of managers. The article can be found at **GiveMore.com/Google**.

Checking email 3 times daily helped us see...

- » Our addiction to checking email (and we cheated ourselves occasionally).
- » It became a default task (automatically checking it when returning from a discussion, meeting, trip to the bathroom, etc.).
- » We sometimes used it to hide out from our more important work ("If I'm addressing email, I'm doing something. It may not be important in the long term but at least I'm of use at this moment." Not good thinking.).
- » Our email can wait and as the day comes to an end, we're more productive and happier (although the first few days were very uncomfortable and ironically had us distracted by our lack of distraction).
- » We weren't as important as we thought we were.

Our customer service people check email hourly in order to be sure we're addressing customer needs quickly. We don't believe we've lost any sales and we've had no negative feedback on our response times.

Focus leads to better results. Two articles on the value of focus I find very inspiring…

> » "The Web Shatters Focus, Rewires Brains" by Nicholas Carr (Wired Magazine), online at **GiveMore.com/Wired**.

> » "Solitude and Leadership" by William Deresiewicz (The American Scholar), online at **GiveMore.com/Solitude**. This one will encourage you to go deeper.

Speaking of more truth … Do you know the fable "The Emperor's New Clothes"? I always thought I did but it really goes much further than I knew (10-minute read, tops).

It's about truth, conviction, and being valuable.

Read with an English accent and a bit of actor's energy, you might find yourself laughing out loud with pity as you recognize the similarities to some of our organizational experiences today. Download a free copy at **GiveMore.com/Truth**.

Pursuit goes beyond just goals and objectives (which are important, of course). For more on this, I love Mike Myatt's thoughts (and reminders) at **GiveMore.com/Pursuit** (on Forbes.com).

Springsteen's spark is a lyric from his song, "Dancing In The Dark" (Born In The U.S.A. – 1984. Columbia Records).

Parents ... Have you noticed how well the Model. Connect. Involve. framework might work with the development of your kids? I've found the more I hold to it, the better the impact seems to be. (More to come.)

King's statement at the end is from one of my favorite books, "Strength to Love." It's a collection of some of his most important sermons and talks. It's faith-based and heavy reading for my brain so it's a great mental workout.

ONE MORE (EXTREMELY IMPORTANT) THOUGHT

All of this assumes you've hired well to begin with and not gomo'd it or wished someone in because you were tired of looking for a solid person and forgot that bringing in the wrong person can cost you more time, money, and people (and pain) in the long run (solid people don't enjoy gomos or d-grunts and might start looking to invest their time elsewhere if their patience runs out).

Most leaders with a little experience know that attitude is an incredibly important evaluation point when looking for the right person (team player, service-oriented, results-focused, positive, enthusiastic, etc.). For some ideas on how to talk with people during the hiring process and learn where their attitude is, you might find my article at **GiveMore.com/Hire** helpful.

And when you find that match, be sure to make their arrival experience a positive one and set expectations high.

ABOUT THE AUTHOR...

I co-founded Give More Media in early 1998. We're a committed group of people in Richmond, Virginia that create things like this book. Our purpose: Encourage and help people make good things happen.

Before Give More, I sold products and services for a little more than a decade in several different industries - financial services, pharmaceuticals, joint replacements, office products, and software.

I wrote the bestselling books 212° the extra degree® (how a little extra effort and attention can make all the difference) and Smile & Move® (a reminder to happily serve). I write often (sign up for our newsletter at **GiveMore.com**), speak to groups and organizations, have a degree in business from James Madison University, and do my best to Lead Simply every day.

You can reach me at Sam@GiveMore.com.
If you're slightly more daring, please call me at (804) 762-4500 ext. 303.

To connect with me in various places on the web, please visit **GiveMore.com/Connect**.

GRATITUDE...

Everything we learn begins with the work of other people.

Thank you to my favorite doers, world changers, leaders, writers, teachers, speakers, and philosophers:

Jesus, Gandhi, Teresa, King, Adams, Franklin, Lincoln, Roosevelts, Churchill, Emerson, Frankl, Edison, Einstein, Disney, Jobs, Gates, Branson, Winfrey, Stewart, Ash, Wise, Pickford, Ball, Presley, Cash, Lennon, McCartney, Jagger, Springsteen, Lucas, Coppola, Spielberg, Hubbard, Carnegie, Peters, Covey, Rohn, Ziglar, Blanchard, Tracy, Godin, Lewis, de Mello, Coelho, Collins, Gladwell, Livingston, Hanh, and so many more.

Mentors and friends: Rich, Jim, Christophe, Leo, Kevin, Pig and her man, Steve, Anthony, Jim, Dad, and My Lady.

Give More People: today's team and those now giving more elsewhere, our customers, our subscribers.

MORE BY SAM...

Most of what I've written is available only at **GiveMore.com**. All of it can be read in less than 30 minutes (some of it in less than 5 minutes).

While each book/ booklet can be enjoyed personally, we've expanded much of the work to include professional development and training material that's used by thousands of people at some of the world's largest and best known organizations. Many of our messages are also very popular within healthcare and education (from K – 12 through the collegiate level).

Our customers have included people at Nike, Gap, Wal-Mart, Verizon, Hershey, Disney, Comcast, the U.S. Olympic Committee, NASCAR, NBC/Universal, NBC/Telemundo, Bank of America, Ernst & Young, New York Life, McDonald's, Tiffany, Target, United Airlines, two branches of the U.S. military, and hundreds of schools and healthcare systems.

 **the extra degree**®

212 (two-twelve) is a clear and powerful message that reminds us and holds us accountable to the fact that a little extra effort and attention can have a big impact on results. It begins with the premise…

At 211 degrees, water is hot. At 212 degrees, it boils.
And with boiling water, comes steam.
And with steam, you can power a train.

Just one extra degree makes all the difference.

Learn more and enjoy the video at
GiveMore.com/212.

smile & move®

This is my follow-up message to 212. It's a reminder to happily serve.

It's all about embracing a positive attitude and taking action.

There are 5 ways to smile (wake up, be thankful, be approachable, complain less, smile more) and 4 ways to move (start early and go long, exceed expectations, have a sense of urgency, be resourceful and resilient).

Learn more and enjoy the video at **GiveMore.com/Smove**.

CROSS THE LINE®

Cross The Line reminds us to commit to go beyond mediocrity in whatever it is we do (no gomos ... people who go through the motions).

It's a fresh way to encourage commitment, effort, focus, and resilience (a 5-minute read, at most). It begins with the fact that...

With everything, there's a line.

On one side of the line, is a greater chance to make good things happen (better results, better relationships, more responsibility). On the other side of the line, there's less of a chance.

And with each line, you have a choice. You want to cross the line or you don't. You want the better chance at making good things happen (meaningful things) or you settle with the lesser chance.

Your choice.

Learn more and enjoy the video at
GiveMore.com/Cross.

LOVE YOUR PEOPLE®

We've let too much get between us (each other) and the reasons we're here.

Love Your People is a declaration of care for those we lead and those we serve. It reminds us to be accountable to each other and make good things happen.

There are 8 principles to Loving Your People (contribute, be kind, be patient, be honest, encourage people, apologize, forgive, thank people).

These are the behaviors that will make things better for everyone. It's a 6-minute read, tops.

Learn more and enjoy the video at
GiveMore.com/Love.

" ALMOST ALWAYS THE **CREATIVE, DEDICATED MINORITY** HAS MADE THE WORLD BETTER. "

MARTIN LUTHER KING, JR.
Nobel Peace Prize winner

(Be a part of that creative, dedicated minority.)